The Magic School Bus

and the Science Fair Expedition

SCIENCE FAIR
WHAT WILL YOUR PROJECT BE?

OUR FAVORITE SCIENTISTS
GEORGE WASHINGTON CARVER
Agricultural Research
STEPHEN W. HAWKING
Origins of the Universe
GREGOR MENDEL
Laws of Heredity
THAT'S NOT A REAL SCIENTIST!
BUT HE'S FAMOUS!
DR. FRANKENSTEIN
Monster Maker

The Magic School Bus

and the Science Fair Expedition

By Joanna Cole
Illustrated by Bruce Degen

Scholastic Press / New York

Many people have helped in the making of this book. Our gratitude goes to John and Mary Gribbin, for their expert review and wonderfully informed perspective. And to Robin Wasserman, for her keen observations. Thanks to John Helms for his expertise — and for weighing the paper clip! To Warren Hirsch and Steven Vizner for astronomy and radium know-how. To Rachel Cole, Heidi Coffin, Mark Goldman, Erica Goldman, and Chris Santoro for their reading and comments. And to Michael Proia on Peaks Island, Maine, for tweaking Arnold's speech bubble on page 28. Appreciation also goes to our editors Kristin Earhart, and especially Craig Walker, who has been inspiring us from the very start. To Stephanie Calmenson for her wise counsel and pertinent questions. And, always, to our spouses Phil Cole and Chris Degen for their enduring support.

Library of Congress Cataloging-in-Publication Data Available

ISBN 0-590-10824-7

10 9 8 7 6 5 4 3 2 6 7 8 9/0

Printed in Singapore 46
First edition, August 2006

The text type was set in 15-point Bookman Light.
The illustrator used pen and ink, watercolor, color pencil, and gouache for the paintings in this book.

To Stephanie Calmenson,
for her generosity, humor, and advice,
but most of all, for her friendship,
which has so enriched my life.
—J.C.

To my dear family,
at home and abroad,
with the world in their hands,
and the earth between their fingers.
—B.D.

In Ms. Frizzle's class, we really needed help!
We were working on projects for the science fair.
The fair was only a few days away,
but some of us had no idea what to do.

I CAN'T THINK OF A SCIENCE PROJECT.
I CAN'T, EITHER.
WILLIAM SMITH
FATHER OF GEOLOGY
I WAS GOING TO DO ONE ON ANTS, BUT THEY GOT AWAY.
Great Stories About Great Scientists

Then Arnold had a suggestion:
"We could get ideas at the new science museum."
The museum was just around the corner.
We could walk there instead of riding
on our wacky old school bus!

WALKERS
WALKERVILLE SCIENCE MUSEUM
BYE-BYE, BUS!
WITHOUT THAT CRAZY BUS, MS. FRIZZLE CAN'T TAKE US ON A CRAZY TRIP.
WALK THIS WAY, CHILDREN.

Ms. Frizzle led the way through the museum doors.
Inside, there were so many things to see and do.

CLASS, THIS SAYS THAT SCIENCE IS ABOUT TESTING IDEAS.
WITHOUT THE SCIENTIFIC METHOD
Get an idea ⇨ Don't test it ⇨ ⇨ Believe what you want.
Idea: AIR HAS WEIGHT
WE DON'T FEEL ANY WEIGHT.
WE DON'T BELIEVE IT.
I DO.
WHO IS RIGHT?
WE CAN'T TELL.
WITH THE SCIENTIFIC METHOD
Get an idea ⇨ Test it before believing it.
Idea: AIR HAS WEIGHT
LET'S TEST IT.
Weigh a bottle that has air in it.
Pump the air out.
Weigh the bottle again.
It weighs less.
SO THE AIR DOES HAVE WEIGHT.
WE PROVED IT!
DID SHE SAY WE'RE HAVING A TEST?
RIGHT HERE IN THE MUSEUM?
NOT TO WORRY. SHE'S JUST TALKING, I HOPE.

COMING HERE WAS A GREAT IDEA, ARNOLD!
I COULD DO A PROJECT ON MAGNETS.
I COULD DO ONE ON BRIDGES.
BIOSPHERE
O^2
CO^2
MICHAEL FARADAY AND THE ELECTRO-MAGNET
MAGNETIC CHARGE
OPPOSITES ATTRACT
LIKES REPEL
ARCHES
BUT MS. FRIZZLE, WE STILL DON'T HAVE A PROJECT.
COMPLETING A CIRCUIT

Then we saw a big cardboard bus.
We could get our picture taken on it.
We all climbed aboard.

RIDE THE BUS THAT MAKES SCIENCE FUN!
GET YOUR PICTURE TAKEN HERE!
UH-OH. SOMEONE FOUND OUT ABOUT OUR BUS.
RELAX, ARNOLD. IT'S JUST CARDBOARD.
GUARD
JD PHOTOS

The photographer snapped the picture.
His flash went off.
Then, wouldn't you know it?
Ms. Frizzle flicked on the high beams.
There was a bigger flash,
and the cardboard bus started moving.

FLASH
WE'VE BEEN FRIZZLED AGAIN!
IS IT SAFE TO DRIVE A CARDBOARD BUS?
I NEVER THOUGHT I'D MISS OUR OLD BUS.
FLASH

We rolled up to a wide entryway that
led to a show on great scientists.
"Isn't this wonderful, children?" said Ms. Frizzle.
"We're going to learn how scientists work!"

GREAT SCIENTISTS THROUGH THE AGES

WEATHER: FOLLOW EL NIÑO
HOW CAN OCEAN TEMPERATURES START HURRICANES?
VOLCANO! MOUNT VINEGAR
BAKING SODA
VINEGAR
WHAT HAPPENS WHEN YOU ADD VINEGAR TO BAKING SODA?
I JUST KNOW THIS WILL HELP WITH OUR SCIENCE PROJECTS!
I'M GETTING A BAD FEELING ABOUT THIS.
DOESN'T SHE NOTICE THAT THIS BUS IS WEIRD?
IT'S EVEN WEIRDER THAN OUR REAL BUS!
SCIENCE Q & A
by Carlos
Q. What's the first thing you need to be a Scientist?
A. CURIOSITY!
Science began because people asked questions about the world.
HOW?
WHAT?
WHAT IF...?

Inside, we saw life-size models
of famous scientists in history.
Our bus glided past a model of Copernicus.
"This famous scientist said that the planets –
including our Earth – went around the sun,"
said Ms. Frizzle.
"But he could not prove it."

COPERNICUS'S QUESTION:
DOES THE EARTH TRAVEL AROUND THE SUN?
EXHIBIT: PART ONE
The Sun and the Planets
IN THE TIME OF COPERNICUS, MOST PEOPLE THOUGHT THE EARTH WAS THE CENTER AND THE SUN WENT AROUND IT.
THE OLD BELIEF:
SUN
EARTH
TODAY WE KNOW THE SUN IS AT THE CENTER.
COPERNICUS'S BELIEF:
EARTH
SUN
COPERNICUS
Born 1473
Died 1543
I THOUGHT I WAS THE CENTER OF EVERYTHING.
WE NOTICED THAT.

As the bus came up to the model of Galileo, we got a big surprise. The model came to life! Galileo ran over, knocked on the door, and shouted, "I'm about to make an important discovery! I need my telescope! I need a ride home!"

The Friz opened the bus door,
and Galileo hopped on. "You're in luck, Gal,"
said Ms. Frizzle. "We were just leaving."
There was a blinding flash,
and the bus jerked forward.
"Next stop, Italy, four hundred years ago,"
shouted the Friz from the driver's seat.

I KNEW A NICE, BORING TRIP WAS TOO GOOD TO BE TRUE.
BUS, DO YOUR STUFF!
FLASH

A STORY ABOUT GALILEO

He Made a Better One

In the early 1600s, people in Italy had never seen a telescope. Then Galileo heard that a man had brought one to his country.

I'LL MAKE ONE MYSELF!

Galileo wanted to look through the telescope, but it was in another part of Italy. So he made one of his own.

Other people had used telescopes to look at ships or armies. Galileo did what no one had done before. He used his to look at the night sky.

The next thing we knew, the bus had rolled up in front of a tall, narrow house. Galileo went in and came out with a telescope.

CLASS, HERE WE ARE IN THE CITY OF PISA, IN THE YEAR 1610.
WOW! A WHOLE CITY OF PIZZA!
SHE SAID PISA, RALPHIE. NOT PIZZA.
GALILEO

Almost seventy years had passed since Copernicus's death, but many people still didn't believe his idea that the Earth went around the sun.
"I think Copernicus was right!" said Galileo.

A WORD FROM
DOROTHY ANN
EVIDENCE is something that can help prove an idea.
I BELIEVE THERE IS AN ELEPHANT IN THE BATHTUB.
EVIDENCE
WE THINK COPERNICUS WAS WRONG.
BEFORE COPERNICUS
MOON
SUN
EARTH
THE EARTH CAN'T TRAVEL.
BYE-BYE MOON.
IF IT DID, THE MOON AND THE EARTH WOULD DRIFT APART!
I'LL FIND EVIDENCE THAT THE EARTH MOVES.
GO FOR IT, GALILEO!

"I have to show that the Earth can move," said Galileo.
That night, he looked at the sky through his telescope.
We got a chance to look, too.
We saw a big planet with four moons around it.
The planet was Jupiter.

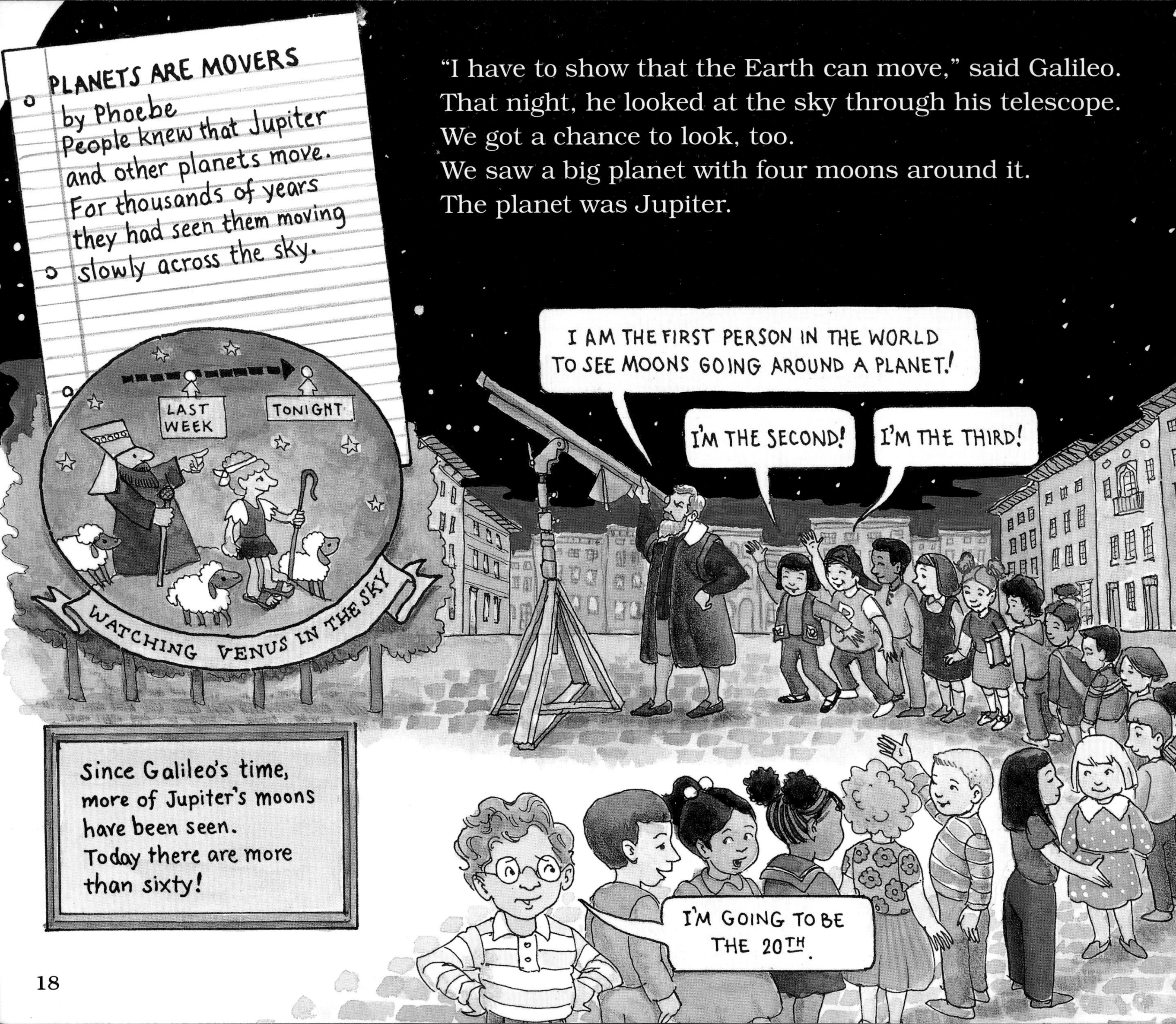

PLANETS ARE MOVERS
by Phoebe
People knew that Jupiter and other planets move. For thousands of years they had seen them moving slowly across the sky.
LAST WEEK
TONIGHT
WATCHING VENUS IN THE SKY
I AM THE FIRST PERSON IN THE WORLD TO SEE MOONS GOING AROUND A PLANET!
I'M THE SECOND!
I'M THE THIRD!
Since Galileo's time, more of Jupiter's moons have been seen. Today there are more than sixty!
I'M GOING TO BE THE 20TH.

Galileo thought hard about his evidence.
Ms. Frizzle told us, "Galileo's discovery
was important, class.
It showed that our Earth and moon could
move together around the sun."

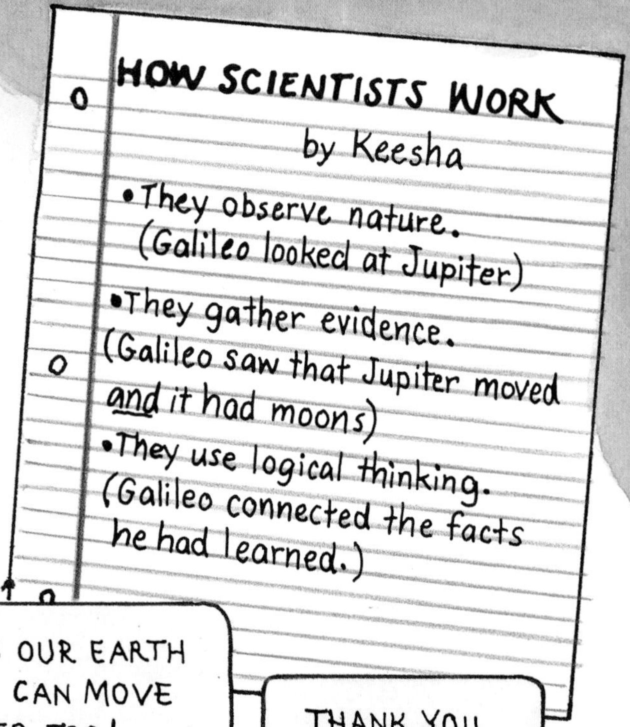
HOW SCIENTISTS WORK
by Keesha
•They observe nature. (Galileo looked at Jupiter)
•They gather evidence. (Galileo saw that Jupiter moved and it had moons)
•They use logical thinking. (Galileo connected the facts he had learned.)

WE HAVE SEEN JUPITER MOVE
AND WE HAVE SEEN ITS MOONS.
THE PLANET AND THE MOONS MOVE TOGETHER.
JUPITER AND ITS MOONS
THAT MEANS OUR EARTH AND MOON CAN MOVE TOGETHER, TOO!
EARTH
MOON
SUN
THANK YOU, GALILEO. NOW WE HAVE TO GET MOVING, OURSELVES.
GALILEO IS OFTEN CALLED THE WORLD'S FIRST MODERN SCIENTIST.

As we were driving away, we met someone
standing in the road and staring into space.
It was not the kind of staring into space
Galileo did with his telescope.
It was the kind that gets you run over
by a cardboard bus.
The man was Isaac Newton.

MS. FRIZZLE, WATCH OUT FOR THAT MAN!
ISAAC NEWTON, YOU ARE IN THE WRONG TIME AND PLACE.
LET'S TAKE HIM HOME.
SCREECH
Sir Isaac Newton
Born 1642
Died 1727

Newton climbed aboard.
Ms. Frizzle flicked on her brights
and . . . *FLASH!* The bus took off!

FLASH

In an instant, we were on a farm in England.
Just like that, it was fifty-five years later.
Newton stepped off the bus
and sat under an apple tree.

NEWTON'S QUESTION:
WHAT KEEPS THE PLANETS IN THEIR ORBITS?
HE'S JUST SITTING THERE.
IF HE'S SUCH A BIG SHOT SCIENTIST, SHOULDN'T HE BE DOING AN EXPERIMENT?
DON'T WORRY, CLASS. HE'S THINKING.
SON, DON'T LET THOSE COWS WANDER OFF.
ANOTHER WORD FROM DOROTHY ANN
An orbit is the path of an object– like the Earth– around another object– like the sun.
SUN
EARTH
ORBIT

A STORY ABOUT NEWTON

Home from College

In 1665, while Newton was studying at Cambridge University, a terrible disease called the plague broke out.

The university sent all the students home, so they wouldn't get sick. Newton returned to his family farm.

HO-HUM!
HOE

While at home, he discovered many things. The most important was that the laws of motion on Earth are the same laws that control the motion of the whole universe. This idea is called Newton's Law of Universal Gravitation.

THERE GO THE COWS.
AHA!

Ms. Frizzle said Isaac was thinking about
the Earth and the moon.
Thump! Isaac saw an apple fall off the tree.
"Hmm," he said. "I know that the apple
was pulled by Earth's gravity.
If gravity's pull can reach to the top of the tree,
maybe it can reach as far as the moon."

THAT'S JUST SILLY!
THE PLANETS AND MOONS ARE NOT LIKE APPLES!
WHAT HAPPENS IN THE SKY HAS NOTHING TO DO WITH WHAT HAPPENS ON EARTH!

Now Newton began thinking about the sun and planets. He told us, “The sun’s gravity holds the planets and their moons in orbit.”

HOW GRAVITY MAKES ORBITS
by Keesha

Keesha is like the Earth.
The string is like gravity.
The ball is like the moon.

WHIRL THE BALL (moon) ON THE STRING (gravity). THEN LET IT GO!

WITHOUT “GRAVITY,” THE “MOON” FLIES AWAY.

ORBIT
GRAVITY IS THE “GLUE” THAT HOLDS THE UNIVERSE TOGETHER!
NEWTON’S THOUGHTS: (Lots of ideas. No cows.)
SUN
SUN AND PLANETS
WE’D BETTER CATCH THOSE COWS.
NEWTON IS SUPPOSED TO BE WATCHING THEM.
HE CAN’T— HE’S THINKING TOO HARD.

MORE ON HOW SCIENTISTS WORK
by Tim

They often prove things by describing them mathematically.
(Newton did his math homework.)

NEWTON
GALILEO
COPERNICUS
NEWTON BUILT ON THE WORK OF OTHERS.

Newton wanted to prove his ideas. He was able to do that using math. Math is the language that scientists use to describe the universe.

NEWTON'S LAW OF UNIVERSAL GRAVITATION
$\frac{g\ moon}{g\ apple} = \frac{0.00272\ m/s^2}{9.8\ m/s^2} = \frac{1}{3600}$
CLASS, NEWTON'S MATH IS VERY ADVANCED.
SOMEDAY, I'LL EXPLAIN IT TO YOU, MS. FRIZZLE.
YOU DID A GOOD JOB WITH THE COWS, ISAAC.

FLASH

We thanked Newton and piled into the bus.
Ms. Frizzle called from the driver's seat,
"Copernicus, Galileo, and Newton
studied something very big – the universe!
Let's meet scientists who study *small* things."
She flicked her brights.
In a flash, we were in Holland!

THERE ARE SOME SMALL TULIPS.
THOSE WOODEN SHOES ARE PRETTY SMALL.
OH, WE'RE LOOKING FOR THINGS MUCH SMALLER THAN THAT.
WE'RE GOING TO SEE ANTONI VAN LEEUWENHOEK.
LEEUWENHOEK
ANTONI VAN LAY-VEN-WHO?
THAT SHOP OVER THERE MUST BELONG TO HIM.
HOW TO SAY LEEUWENHOEK:
LAY-VEN-HOOK

A STORY ABOUT ANTONI VAN LEEUWENHOEK

Looking at Threads

Antoni van Leeuwenhoek was a draper — a seller of cloth. But he was interested in a lot more than cloth. One day he saw a book by an English scientist named Robert Hooke. There were drawings of things Hooke had seen under a microscope. Antoni was amazed.

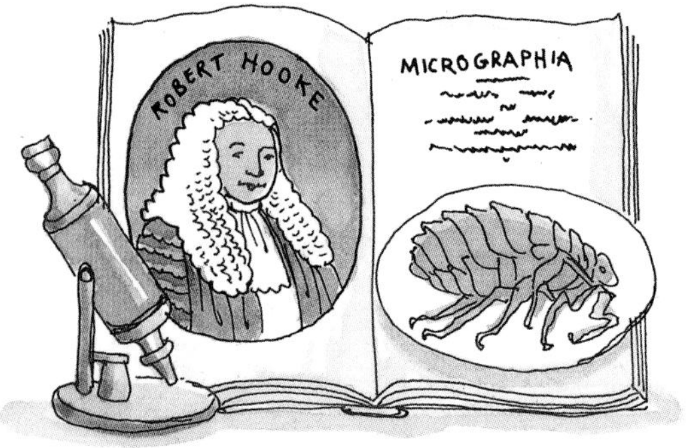
ROBERT HOOKE
MICROGRAPHIA

Antoni knew about magnifiers. Every day he used a magnifying glass to make sure the threads in his cloth were straight and tight. He decided to build his own microscope.

We went into Leeuwenhoek's cloth shop.
There he was at the window,
peering into an odd little microscope.
LEEUWENHOEK'S MICROSCOPE DOESN'T LOOK LIKE THE ONES WE USUALLY SEE.
HIS HAIRSTYLE DOESN'T LOOK LIKE THE ONES WE USUALLY SEE, EITHER.
IN LEEUWENHOEK'S DAY, MEN WORE WIGS, ARNOLD.
ANTONI VAN LEEUWENHOEK
Born 1632–Died 1723

Leeuwenhoek's microscope was so good that he saw things no one else could see.

LEEUWENHOEK'S QUESTION:
ARE THERE LIVING THINGS SO TINY THAT WE CAN'T SEE THEM WITH JUST OUR EYES?
I'M LOOKING AT A DROP OF WATER. I CAN SEE LITTLE ANIMALS SWIMMING ALL AROUND.
LEEUWENHOEK WAS THE FIRST TO SEE THESE TINY LIVING THINGS.
WHY IS THAT IMPORTANT?
BECAUSE AFTER LEEUWENHOEK A WHOLE NEW SCIENCE WAS STARTED. IT WAS CALLED MICROBIOLOGY.
ONE MORE WORD FROM DOROTHY ANN
Microbiology is the science of tiny animals and plants.
LEEUWENHOEK IS CALLED THE FATHER OF MICROBIOLOGY.
HE'S OUR DAD!
FUNGI
BACTERIA
LENS
SPECIMEN ON GLASS SLIDE
ALGAE
FOCUS SCREW
LEEUWENHOEK'S MICROSCOPE
LENS
FOCUS KNOB
BACTERIA
SPECIMEN ON GLASS SLIDE
ANOTHER LENS
MODERN MICROSCOPE

"I've spent fifty years looking at things," said Leeuwenhoek. "I'm curious about everything." When he said "everything," he really meant it. It could get kind of gross.

I AM SCRAPING THIS SOFT WHITE STUFF FROM MY TEETH.

STILL MORE WAYS SCIENTISTS WORK
by Wanda
They use their hands as well as their heads.
(Van Leeuwenhoek worked carefully to build his own microscopes.)

THESE ARE EXCELLENT LENSES, ANTONI.
THANKS, I GRIND THEM MYSELF.

LOOK! THERE ARE LITTLE ANIMALS IN IT.
EEUW!
HASN'T HE EVER HEARD OF FLOSSING?
The "little animals" Leeuwenhoek saw in dental plaque were actually bacteria.

"We're out of here!" we yelled, and we raced to the bus.

THANK YOU, ANTONI VAN LEEUWENHOEK! YOU SHOWED US A WORLD OF TINY THINGS ALL AROUND US AND IN US.
THANK YOU, MS. FRIZZLE. YOU HELPED US ESCAPE FROM THAT TINY AND DISGUSTING WORLD.

Ms. Frizzle flashed the brights . . .

. . . and we landed in France . . . *HARD!*

HOW CAN A CARDBOARD BUS GET A FLAT TIRE?
IS THERE A CARDBOARD SPARE?
BAM!

A STORY ABOUT LOUIS PASTEUR

Using Science for Health

Louis grew up in a small French town. He was very good in school, went to the best college in France, and became a scientist.

Soon people began to come to him with problems. Winemakers said, "My wine is going bad." Farmers had sick chickens, cows, and sheep. Louis wanted to help them all.

He began asking questions about all the problems. In his lab he found answers that helped make the world a healthier place.

Suddenly, a distinguished gentleman came by. "May I be of help?" he asked.
"Louis Pasteur!" our teacher answered.
"I was hoping you'd come along."
When the tire was fixed, Louis asked us to drive him home.

CLASS, MEET LOUIS PASTEUR. HE MADE MODERN MEDICINE POSSIBLE.
HE'S MAKING CARDBOARD-BUS TRAVEL POSSIBLE!
WHAT AN AMAZING VEHICLE!
GLUE
LOUIS PASTEUR
Born 1822 – Died 1895

We all got on the bus, and Ms. Frizzle
drove us into farm country.
It was beautiful, but many of the farm animals
were sick and dying.
"These animals have a terrible disease called anthrax,"
Pasteur explained. "I am going to work on it.
Please take me to my laboratory in Paris."

PASTEUR'S QUESTION:
WHAT MAKES US SICK?
ABOUT 200 YEARS HAVE PASSED SINCE LEEUWENHOEK FIRST LOOKED AT BACTERIA.
LEEUWENHOEK SAW BACTERIA. BUT HE DIDN'T THINK THEY CAUSED SICKNESS.
I THINK THEY CAN, AND I WANT TO PROVE IT.
TO THE LAB!
CLASS, ISN'T IT WONDERFUL HOW SCIENTIFIC KNOWLEDGE GROWS OVER THE YEARS?
WHAT ARE BACTERIA?
by Shirley
Bacteria are tiny, one-celled living things.
Some cause disease, but most are helpful.
WE CAUSE FOOD POISONING.
WE HELP MAKE CHEESE.
Salmonella enteritidis
Lactobacilli

ANOTHER WORD FROM DOROTHY ANN

A hypothesis is an idea that will be tested by an experiment.

In his lab, Pasteur explained, "People don't know what causes anthrax. They do know that if they take blood from a sick animal and inject it into a healthy one, the healthy animal will always get anthrax."

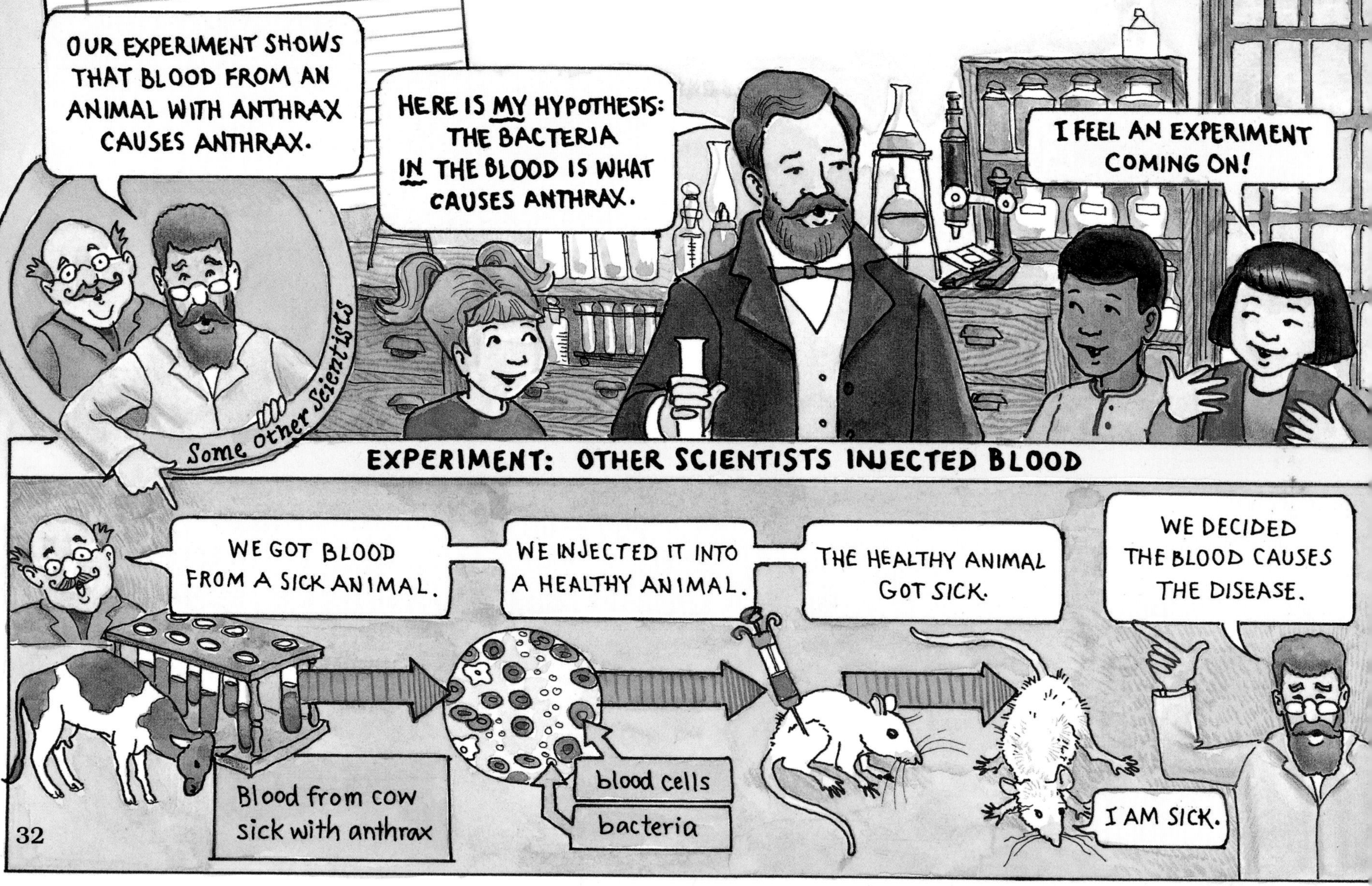

OUR EXPERIMENT SHOWS THAT BLOOD FROM AN ANIMAL WITH ANTHRAX CAUSES ANTHRAX.
Some other Scientists
HERE IS MY HYPOTHESIS: THE BACTERIA IN THE BLOOD IS WHAT CAUSES ANTHRAX.
I FEEL AN EXPERIMENT COMING ON!
EXPERIMENT: OTHER SCIENTISTS INJECTED BLOOD
WE GOT BLOOD FROM A SICK ANIMAL.
WE INJECTED IT INTO A HEALTHY ANIMAL.
THE HEALTHY ANIMAL GOT SICK.
WE DECIDED THE BLOOD CAUSES THE DISEASE.
Blood from cow sick with anthrax
blood cells
bacteria
I AM SICK.

Pasteur carried out a great experiment.
It proved that the bacteria caused anthrax.
Once he knew that, he was able to make
a vaccine that prevented the disease.

HOW SCIENTISTS WORK
by Arnold
They do experiments.
(Pasteur's experiments saved lives.)
WITHOUT A DOUBT, MY EXPERIMENT PROVES MY HYPOTHESIS!
WHY IS THAT IMPORTANT?
BECAUSE IF PEOPLE KNOW THE REAL CAUSE OF A SICKNESS, THEY CAN TRY TO FIND A CURE!
IS THERE A CURE FOR WEIRD TEACHERS?
Scientists build on one another's work
PASTEUR
LEEUWENHOEK
HOOKE
EXPERIMENT: PASTEUR INJECTED BACTERIA
I GOT BLOOD FROM AN ANIMAL THAT HAD ANTHRAX.
blood
bacteria
I TOOK OUT THE BACTERIA.
bacteria
I INJECTED THE BACTERIA ONLY INTO A HEALTHY LAB ANIMAL.
THE ANIMAL GOT ANTHRAX! THIS PROVED THAT THE BACTERIA CAUSED THE DISEASE.
I AM SICK!

FLASH

We filed out of Pasteur's lab and onto the bus.
Ms. Frizzle stepped on the gas, flicked on the brights, and — *FLASH!* — the bus went into action.
When it stopped, we were still in Paris, but we were at another laboratory. It was twenty years later.
"Now we'll meet Marie and Pierre Curie," said the Friz. "They are about to discover something exciting."

WE'LL WEAR THESE SUITS TO PROTECT US FROM THE DANGEROUS RAYS IN THE CURIES' LAB.
DANGEROUS?
LET'S GO BACK TO THE GUY WHO SCRAPED THE GUNK OFF HIS TEETH!

WHAT ARE RAYS?
by Florrie

Rays are thin lines of energy.
There are:

light rays,

heat rays,

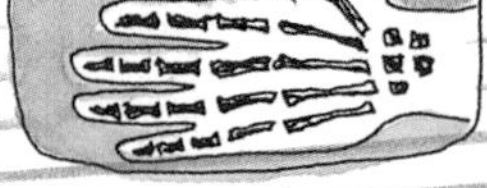
Xrays

and lots of others.

The lab turned out to be a wooden shed. Marie Curie was stirring a big pot over a fire. The stirrer was almost as big as she was! "What's in the pot?" we wondered.

MADAME CURIE, WHY DO YOU WORK IN THIS LEAKY, OLD PLACE?
BECAUSE WOMEN ARE NOT ALLOWED IN THE UNIVERSITY LABS.
WOW, IT MUST HAVE BEEN HARD TO BE A WOMAN SCIENTIST IN THOSE DAYS.
MARIE SKLODOWSKA CURIE
Born 1867 - Died 1934

A STORY ABOUT MARIE CURIE

How She Got to Paris

Marie Curie was a famous scientist who worked in Paris, France. She came there from Poland, and her original name was Marya Sklodowska. Marya loved to learn. But at that time in Poland, girls were not allowed to go to college.

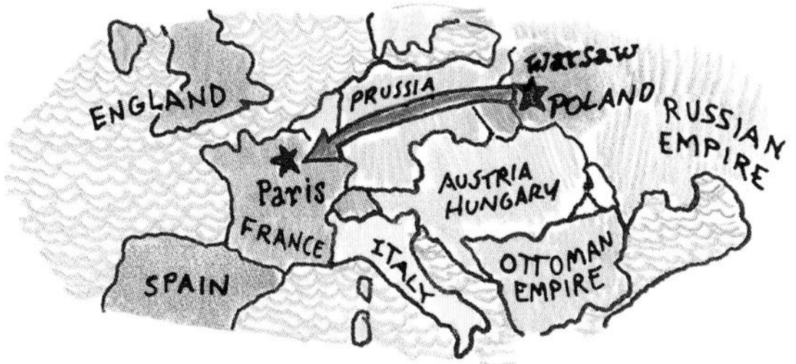

She worked for six years and saved enough money to go to the University of Paris. She was still so poor that she lived in an attic and ate almost nothing but tea and bread.

Marya changed her name to a French name, Marie. Later, when she married Pierre Curie, she changed her last name, too.

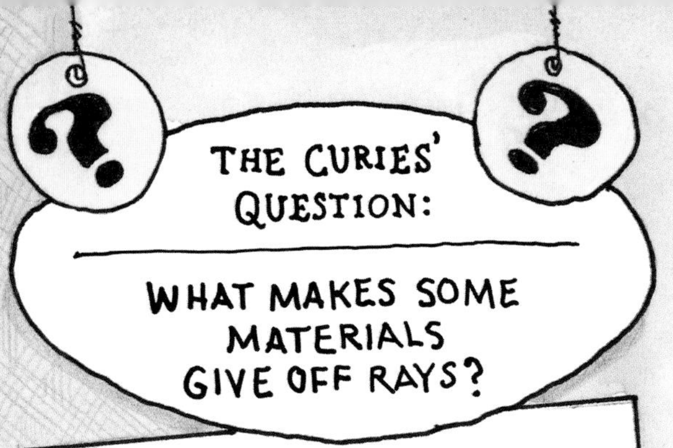

Wanda looked in the pot. "It's just mud," she said.
"This stuff is called pitchblende," said Marie.
"I am trying to find a radioactive material in it."

WHAT IS RADIOACTIVITY?
by Amanda Jane
Some materials are radioactive. That means they give off invisible rays.
When Marie Curie started her work, no one knew what the rays were made of.
I AM ANTOINE HENRI BECQUEREL. IN 1896, I FOUND URANIUM IN PITCHBLENDE. IT WAS THE FIRST RADIOACTIVE ELEMENT TO BE DISCOVERED. MARIE CURIE WANTED TO FIND MORE.
I DON'T REALLY UNDERSTAND RADIOACTIVITY.
JUST WAIT AND WE'LL LEARN ALL ABOUT IT!
WE ALWAYS DO IN MS. FRIZZLE'S CLASS.

Marie's husband, Pierre, was a scientist, too. He became so interested in Marie's research that he gave up his own work and started helping her. Marie and Pierre Curie found a way to take the radioactive matter out of the pitchblende.

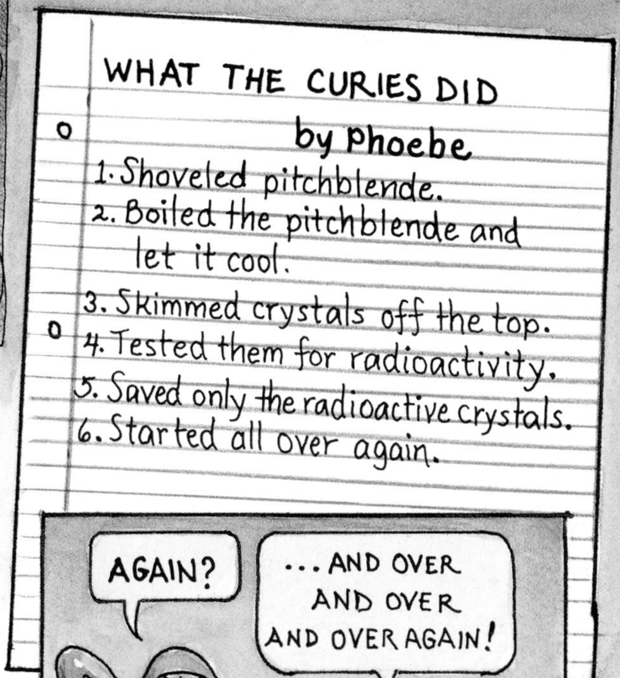
WHAT THE CURIES DID
by Phoebe
1. Shoveled pitchblende.
2. Boiled the pitchblende and let it cool.
3. Skimmed crystals off the top.
4. Tested them for radioactivity.
5. Saved only the radioactive crystals.
6. Started all over again.

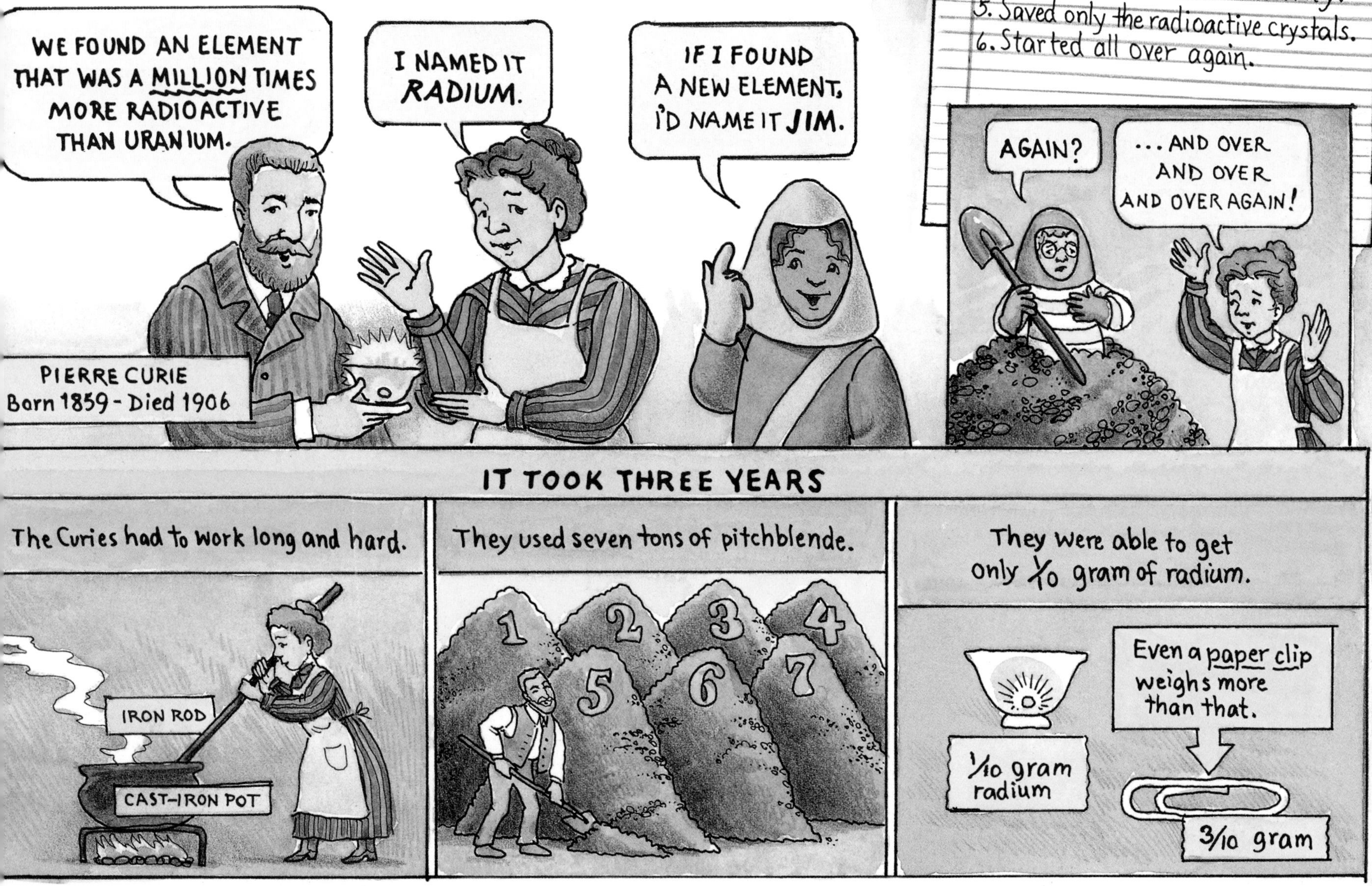
WE FOUND AN ELEMENT THAT WAS A MILLION TIMES MORE RADIOACTIVE THAN URANIUM.
I NAMED IT RADIUM.
IF I FOUND A NEW ELEMENT, I'D NAME IT JIM.
PIERRE CURIE
Born 1859 - Died 1906
AGAIN?
... AND OVER AND OVER AND OVER AGAIN!
IT TOOK THREE YEARS
The Curies had to work long and hard.
IRON ROD
CAST-IRON POT
They used seven tons of pitchblende.
1
2
3
4
5
6
7
They were able to get only 1/10 gram of radium.
1/10 gram radium
Even a paper clip weighs more than that.
3/10 gram

They found just a little bit of radium,
but it helped Marie make a big discovery.
“Marie realized that radioactivity must come
from inside the radium,” said Pierre.
“Radium must be spitting out super-tiny
parts of its atoms,” said Marie.
“When the atomic particles come out,
energy comes out, too.”

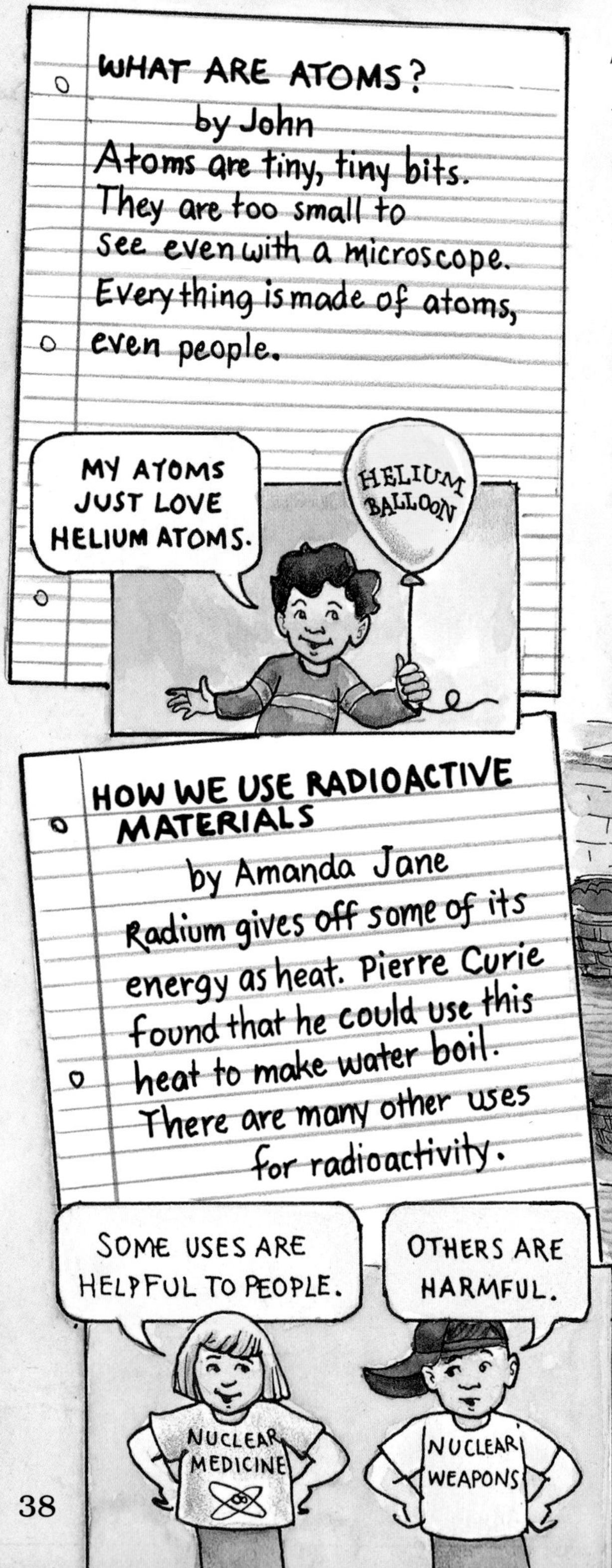

WHAT ARE ATOMS?
by John
Atoms are tiny, tiny bits. They are too small to see even with a microscope. Everything is made of atoms, even people.
MY ATOMS JUST LOVE HELIUM ATOMS.
HELIUM BALLOON
HOW WE USE RADIOACTIVE MATERIALS
by Amanda Jane
Radium gives off some of its energy as heat. Pierre Curie found that he could use this heat to make water boil. There are many other uses for radioactivity.
SOME USES ARE HELPFUL TO PEOPLE.
OTHERS ARE HARMFUL.
NUCLEAR MEDICINE
NUCLEAR WEAPONS

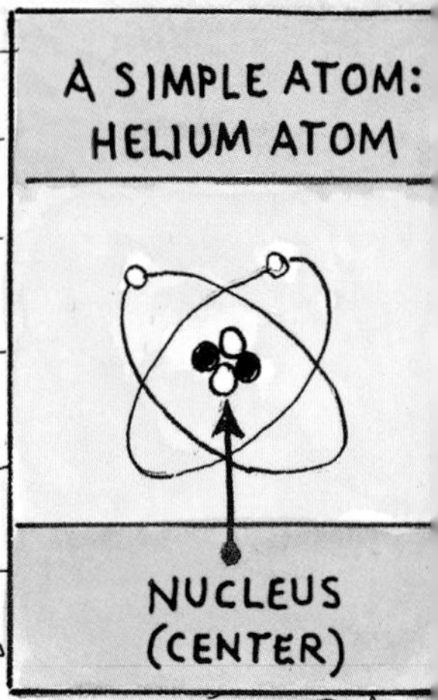

A SIMPLE ATOM: HELIUM ATOM
NUCLEUS (CENTER)

THERE'S ENERGY IN ATOMS!
IT'S ATOMIC ENERGY!
RADIUM GIVES OFF HEAT ENERGY AND LIGHT ENERGY.
WE LOVE TO VISIT THE LAB AT NIGHT.
IT GIVES OFF A BEAUTIFUL BLUE LIGHT.
PIERRE'S EXPERIMENT
A bit of radium in a beaker of water will make the water boil.

Today we know that too much radioactivity is harmful.
But the Curies didn't know that.
Dorothy Ann read from her book:
"They didn't protect themselves.
After a while, they became very sick."

A MORE COMPLEX ATOM:
RADIUM
RADIOACTIVITY:
nucleus of radium atom spits out pieces
OUR SUITS ARE PROTECTING US.
I WISH WE COULD WARN THE CURIES.
BUT MS. FRIZZLE TOLD US THERE IS NO WAY TO CHANGE THE PAST.
CLASS, LET'S THANK THE CURIES AND BE ON OUR WAY.
DANGEROUS NOTEBOOKS
by Tim
Even today, the Curies' notebooks are so radioactive that they are kept in radiation-proof containers.
HOW SCIENTISTS WORK
by Arnold
They put in long hours. (The Curies worked night and day for years to discover radium.)
Sometimes scientists take risks, whether they mean to or not. (The Curies did not know their work was dangerous.)

A STORY ABOUT ALBERT EINSTEIN

A Compass to Play With

One day, when Albert was about five years old, he was sick in bed. His father gave him a compass to play with.

Albert moved the compass all around, but the needle always kept pointing north. He realized that an invisible force was acting on the needle.

N
W
E
S

Einstein's life's work was to find out about the hidden forces of the universe.

We waved good-bye and went outside.
A passenger was sitting quietly
at the very back of the cardboard bus.
It was Albert Einstein,
the most famous scientist ever!

MAY I RIDE WITH YOU, MS. FRIZZLE? I HAVE TO GET TO MY APPOINTMENT AT THE WALKERVILLE SCIENCE MUSEUM.
YES, ALBERT! WE'RE GOING THERE OURSELVES.
OH, NO! NOT ANOTHER STRANGE HAIRSTYLE!
POLONIUM
RADIUM
POLONIUM
RADIUM

Then Ms. Frizzle flashed the lights, and the bus took off! As we traveled, Einstein told us about his work. "Most people have heard of my famous mathematical formula, $E = mc^2$," he said. "But many don't know what it means."

$E = mc^2$ EXPLAINS THAT MATTER AND ENERGY ARE REALLY FORMS OF THE SAME THING.
"MATTER CAN CHANGE TO ENERGY, AND ENERGY CAN CHANGE TO MATTER".
THAT'S WHAT HAPPENED IN THE CURIES' LAB!
YES, RADIUM—WHICH IS MATTER—CHANGED INTO HEAT AND LIGHT—WHICH ARE ENERGY!

A LAST WORD FROM DOROTHY ANN

Matter is all of the stuff in the universe, such as plants, pencils, pennies, and cats.

WHAT $E = mc^2$ DOES
by Phil

* It tells how the sun makes heat and light.
* It explains radioactivity.
* It tells how the universe began.

DID YOU KNOW?

IF THE MASS OF 100 PENNIES WERE CHANGED TO PURE ENERGY, IT COULD POWER NEW YORK STATE FOR TWO DAYS.
SCIENTISTS JUST DON'T KNOW HOW TO DO THAT YET.
ONE CENT
ONE CENT

The bus zoomed to the science museum,
bumped up the steps, rolled through the doors,
and stopped at Einstein's spot in the exhibit.
He stepped into place just in time.
No one had missed him yet.

Einstein said,
"The important thing is
never to stop questioning."

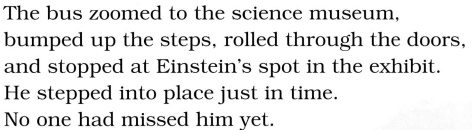

OUR CLASS WILL UNDERSTAND YOUR IDEAS WHEN THEY ARE OLDER, ALBERT.
MUCH OLDER!
TAKE YOUR TIME. IT TOOK ME A WHILE TO UNDERSTAND THEM MYSELF!
EVEN MS. FRIZZLE CAN'T EXPLAIN EINSTEIN TO US.
EVEN EINSTEIN CAN'T EXPLAIN YOUR BUS TO ME!
ALBERT EINSTEIN Born 1879 Died 1955
GUARD
EINSTEIN'S IDEAS CHANGED HOW WE SEE THE UNIVERSE
by Phoebe
Einstein had many amazing ideas — not just $E=mc^2$.
Many of them seem impossible, but they have been proved by experiments and math.
His work inspired other scientists to ask new questions.
What is SPACE-TIME?
What is RELATIVITY?
What is the FABRIC of the UNIVERSE?
WHAT IS FOR LUNCH?

THERE'S CARLOS AND PHOEBE AND TIM AND ISAAC NEWTON...
...AND GALILEO AND ARNOLD AND MARIE CURIE.
THAT'S ONE BUSLOAD OF GREAT MINDS.

WE STILL HAVE TO DO OUR SCIENCE FAIR PROJECTS.
WALK THIS WAY, CHILDREN.

Then our teacher drove over
to the photographer.
Our picture was ready.
It was amazing.
Everyone was in it —
even the scientists!
It must have been magic.

Back at school, everyone got busy.
We all had great questions to ask, such as:
"How do you make a compass?"
"How do plants get water?"
and "What pattern will be on
Ms. Frizzle's dress tomorrow?"

OUR CLASS SCIENCE FAIR
NUMBER TEN?
SOLAR SYSTEM
SUN
How Many Planets Orbit Our Sun?
INSPIRED BY GALILEO and NEWTON
by Carlos
For years, we thought there were nine planets, including Pluto.
But now scientists have found what might be a new planet far beyond the others.

I KNEW VISITING THE SCIENTISTS WOULD INSPIRE US!
WATER
SUGAR
How Is Making Rock Candy Like Separating Radium From Pitchblende?
INSPIRED BY MARIE and PIERRE CURIE
by Keesha
Boil the sugar and water. Then let it cool.
The sugar forms crystals, and that's rock candy.
(VERY HOT ~ requires adult supervision!)

But the most important question
in Ms. Frizzle's class is always:
"Will we ever go on a normal school trip?"

SCIENCE
IS ABOUT ASKING QUESTIONS
AND TESTING IDEAS!
I FOUND MY ANTS! NOW I CAN DO MY PROJECT!
SCIENCE ISN'T JUST ABOUT WHAT WE KNOW...
IT'S ABOUT WHAT WE DON'T KNOW...YET.
LEMONS
SOUR PICKLES
POND WATER
BOILED POND WATER
ELEMENTARY EINSTEIN From Hair to There
Do Ants Like Sweet Things?
by Ralphie
INSPIRED BY CANDY
(which I like!)
Does Boiling Pond Water
Get Rid of Germs?
INSPIRED BY LEEUWENHOEK and PASTEUR
by Wanda
1. Fill jar with water from a pond.
2. Look at drop under microscope.
3. Boil water and let cool.
4. Look at a drop under microscope.

Joanna and Bruce Visit

WE SCIENTISTS HAVE COMPLAINTS ABOUT YOUR BOOK.
COPERNICUS
A CLASS CAN'T REALLY GO BACK IN TIME.
LEEUWENHOEK
I DIDN'T REALLY SIT UNDER AN APPLE TREE. THAT'S JUST A STORY.
ISAAC NEWTON
I ASKED A LOT MORE QUESTIONS THAN THE ONES YOU SHOWED.
GALILEO GALILEI
I DISCOVERED HOW TO MAKE MILK SAFE TO DRINK. YOU LEFT THAT OUT, TOO.
MILK
LOUIS PASTEUR
PIERRE AND I FOUND THREE RADIOACTIVE ELEMENTS. YOU TOLD ABOUT ONLY ONE OF THEM.
PIERRE and MARIE CURIE
UH-OH! BRUCE, THE SCIENTISTS ARE COMPLAINING.
TELL THEM IT'S TOO LATE TO MAKE CHANGES, JOANNA.

the Gallery of Scientists

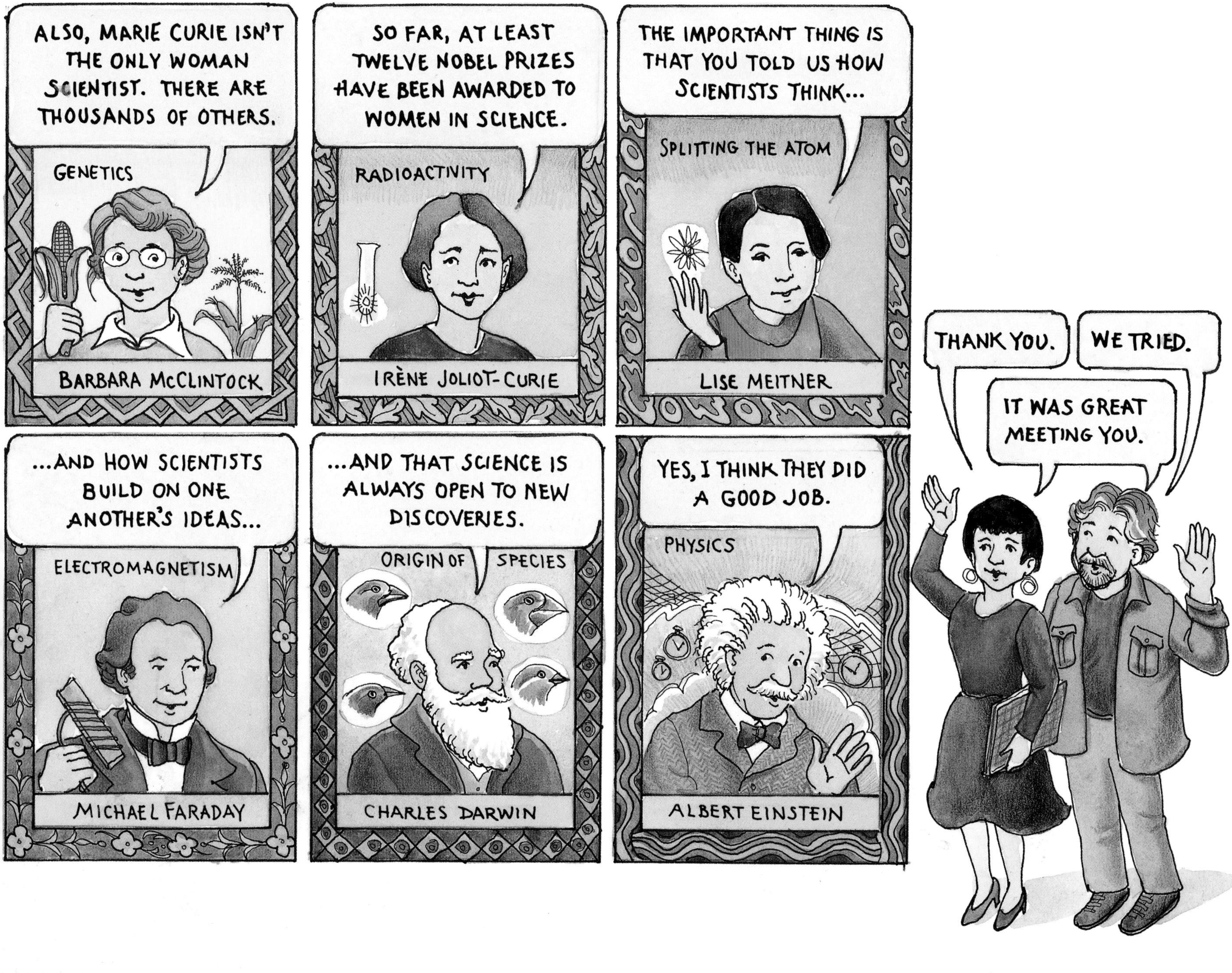

ALSO, MARIE CURIE ISN'T THE ONLY WOMAN SCIENTIST. THERE ARE THOUSANDS OF OTHERS.
GENETICS
BARBARA MCCLINTOCK
SO FAR, AT LEAST TWELVE NOBEL PRIZES HAVE BEEN AWARDED TO WOMEN IN SCIENCE.
RADIOACTIVITY
IRÈNE JOLIOT-CURIE
THE IMPORTANT THING IS THAT YOU TOLD US HOW SCIENTISTS THINK...
SPLITTING THE ATOM
LISE MEITNER
...AND HOW SCIENTISTS BUILD ON ONE ANOTHER'S IDEAS...
ELECTROMAGNETISM
MICHAEL FARADAY
...AND THAT SCIENCE IS ALWAYS OPEN TO NEW DISCOVERIES.
ORIGIN OF SPECIES
CHARLES DARWIN
YES, I THINK THEY DID A GOOD JOB.
PHYSICS
ALBERT EINSTEIN
THANK YOU.
WE TRIED.
IT WAS GREAT MEETING YOU.

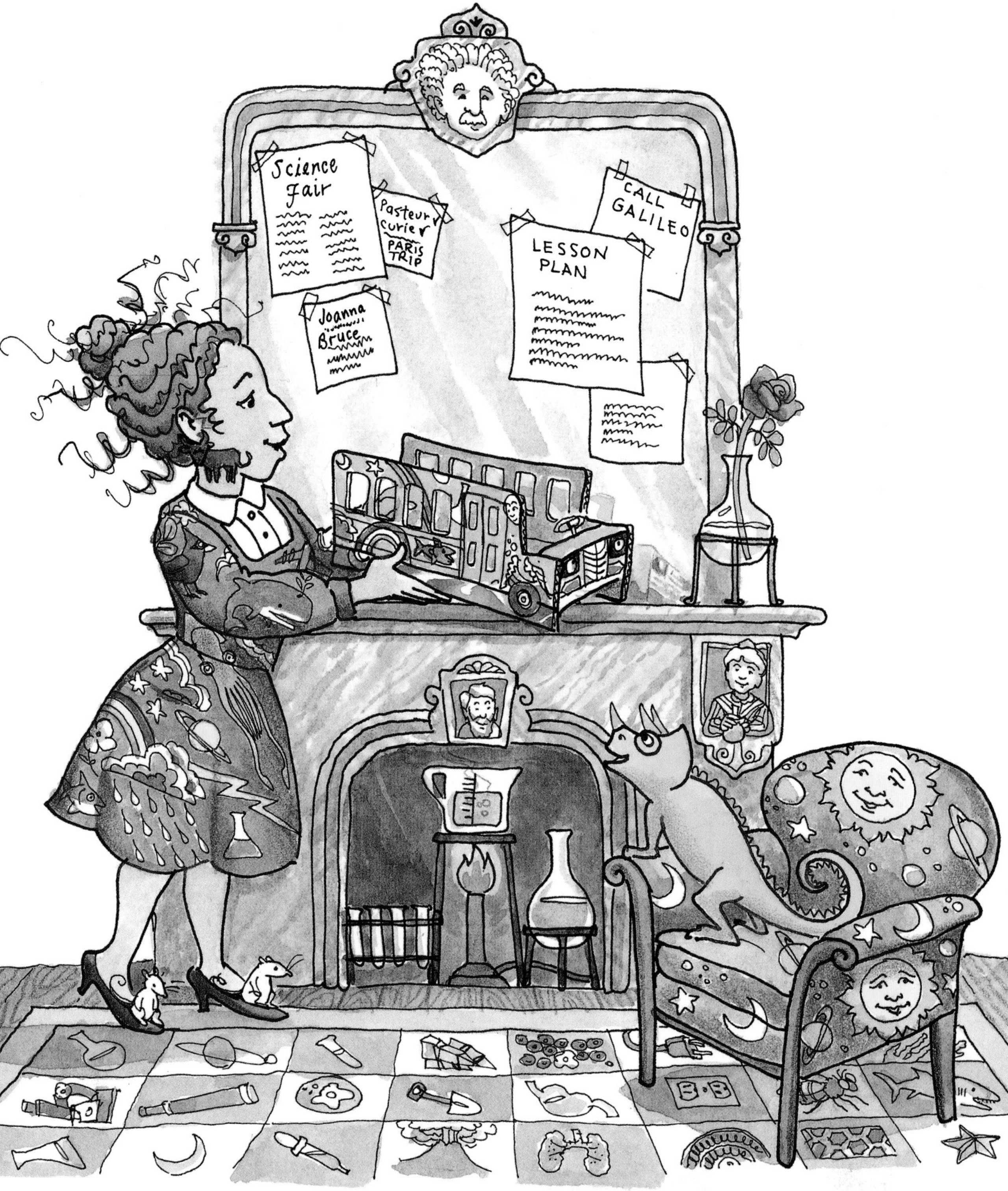
Science Fair
Pasteur
Curie
PARIS TRIP
CALL GALILEO
LESSON PLAN
Joanna
Bruce